SUSAN & MIKEY
AN
ARCADE ADVENTURE
By: Gerdasha Bell

Copyright © 2023 by: Gerdasha Bell
Publisher: Poitier Wordsmith Academy…
Poitier Publishing Company
All rights reserved. No part of this book may be reproduced or transmitted in any form or by any means, electronic or mechanical, including photocopying, recording, or by any information storage and retrieval system, without permission in writing from the author or publisher.

ISBN: 9798396953796
Printed in the United States of America

Susan and Mikey have been best friends since the 1st grade. They enjoy spending time together.

Today, they are going to the mall to play at the new arcade. Mikey was so excited that after school Friday, he told the whole school.

Susan had a huge slice of pizza before they left the house.

Mikey had nothing before leaving the house and he warned Susan not to eat too much so she would be able to ride the dirt bikes at the new arcade. Pizza is her favorite food so he knew she would eat a lot.

Susan reminded Mikey to eat, but he continued to watch tv. Mikey also invited their classmate, Austin to meet them at the new arcade to join the fun.

Mikey was too excited about leaving home to go to the new arcade to eat. He had a special drink the night before to fill him up.

On the way to the mall, Susan was teasing Mikey about not eating. She told him that "juice" could not fill him up. Mikey told Susan it was not juice, it was a "smoothie."

"Mikey I am not going to buy you anything to eat while we are out," said Susan's mom before she dropped them off.

Mikey is just happy to be going to the arcade. He told them again that his smoothie made him full.

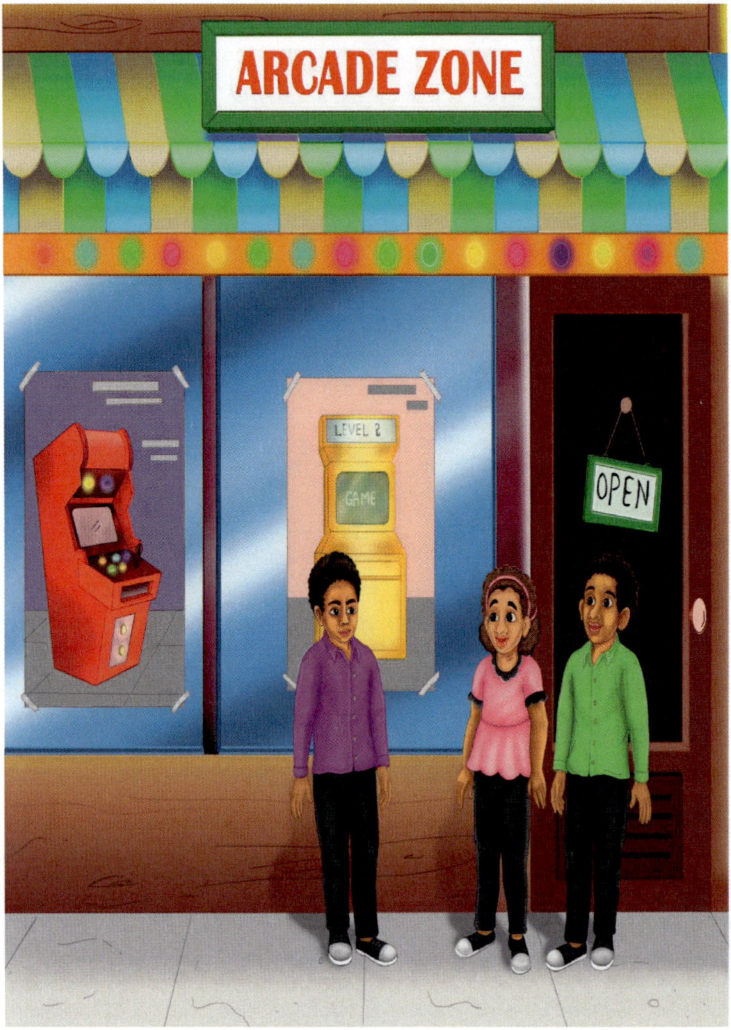
ARCADE ZONE
LEVEL 2
GAME
OPEN

They finally got to the new arcade and Mikey and Susan were so happy to be there. Austin was waiting for them outside.

They played for hours. Austin and Mikey played against each other.

Susan had to sit down for a moment because her stomach was hurting, and she felt ill. She had cramps and felt like she was going to throw up.

Mikey was happy he did not eat because that is what made Susan have problems with her stomach. Austin and Mikey felt good, so they kept playing games.

Even though Susan was sick, she and Mikey had the time of their life at the new arcade and could not wait to return! Austin and Mikey used their winning tickets and bought Susan a gift to make her feel better.

The End of Susan & Mikey's Day at the Arcade…

Made in the USA
Columbia, SC
07 August 2023